Mini Cakes

Mini Cakes

This edition published in 2011

LOVE FOOD is an imprint of Parragon Books Ltd

Parragon
Queen Street House
4 Queen Street
Bath BA1 1HE, UK

ISBN: 978-1-4454-5223-4

Printed in China

Created and produced by Pene Parker and Becca Spry
Author and home economist: Joanna Farrow
Photographer: Noel Murphy

Notes for the reader

This book uses metric, imperial, and US measurements. Follow the same units of measurements
throughout; do not mix metric and imperial. All spoon measurements are level: teaspoons are
assumed to be 5 ml, and tablespoons are assumed to be 15 ml. Unless otherwise stated, milk is
assumed to be whole, eggs are large, individual vegetables are medium, and pepper is freshly
ground black pepper.

The times given are an approximate guide only. Preparation times differ according to the
techniques used by different people and the cooking times may also vary from those given.
Optional ingredients, variations, or serving suggestions have not been included in the calculations.

Recipes using raw or very lightly cooked eggs should be avoided by infants, the elderly, pregnant
women, convalescents, and anyone with a chronic illness. Pregnant and breast-feeding women
are advised to avoid eating peanuts and peanut products. People with nut allergies should be
aware that some of the prepared ingredients used in the recipes in this book may contain nuts.
Always check the packaging before use.

Contents

Introduction

Tiny portions of our favorite treats are so much fun to bake and eat. They're in great demand, perhaps because they have the "cute factor" that large portions don't, or because they're so easy to pop into our mouths. From tiny little fruit loaves to miniature wedding cakes, this book of bite-size morsels offers something for every occasion.

Equipment

A minimal amount of baking equipment is needed to make the cakes in this book. What you don't have already is widely available from cake-decorating stores or via the Internet.

Mini cupcake and muffin cases

Mini cupcake liners and muffin baking cups tend to vary considerably in size. The recipes in this book require paper liners with a bottom diameter of 1¼ inches/3 cm and 1½ inches/4 cm. Mini silicone cups are also available in a variety of colors, from subtle to bright. They're dishwasher-proof and reusable, and cakes are easy to remove from them by peeling away the cups. To bake, simply set the silicone cups on a baking sheet instead of in a muffin pan. Neither silicone cups nor paper liners need greasing.

Mini muffin pans

Paper cupcake liners and muffin baking cups must sit comfortably in the pan's sections, which should offer some support but not crease up the paper liners. Mini muffin pans have 12 or 24 sections; if using a 12-section pan, you will need to bake two batches of cakes for some recipes in this book.

Mini loaf pans

Mini loaves can be made in a 12-section silicone loaf pan with sections measuring 3 x 1½ inches/7 x 3 cm. Alternatively, they can be made in individual metal pans, but these are usually slightly larger, so you won't make as many cakes as the recipe states and you will need a little extra baking time. Silicone pans don't need lining, but line each metal pan with a wide strip of parchment paper that fits over the bottom and up the long sides.

Mini sectioned cake pans

Both round- and square-section cake pans measure 2 inches/5 cm in diameter per section and are usually bought in packages of 16, which fit onto a base for baking. Alternatively, bake a large yellow cake and let it firm up for 24 hours, then cut out 2-inch/5-cm rounds or squares, using a metal cutter as a guide.

Metal cookie cutters

Cookie cutters can be used to cut out shapes from yellow cakes, such as the moons on page 60. Cutters are available in a variety of shapes and sizes and are sometimes sold seasonally, so it's worth collecting your favorite shapes when you see them.

Small square cake pans

A 7-inch/18-cm square cake pan is a useful size for baking a yellow cake to cut into small cakes. Grease and line the bottom and sides of the pan before baking.

Baking techniques

Preparing pans
Use wax paper or parchment paper to line pans and melted butter or vegetable oil to grease them.

Lining square pans
Place the pan on parchment paper, draw around the pan, and cut out the paper just inside the lines. Cut a strip the depth of the pan and long enough to fit around the perimeter of the pan, then make a ½-inch/1-cm fold along one long edge. Grease the pan, using a pastry brush, and fit the strip around the sides so the folded strip sits on the bottom. Snip the folded edge at the corners. Press the paper square into the bottom and grease the paper.

Lining round sectioned pans
Grease the sections. Cut out circles of parchment paper ½ inch/1 cm larger than the section diameters. Make ¼ inch/5 mm cuts at the sides of the circles and press them in sections so the snipped edges go up the sides.

Mixing muffins
Muffins are made by adding the wet ingredients to the dry ingredients. The flour is usually sifted first. Add the wet ingredients all at once and fold everything together gently. As soon as they're combined but with specks of flour still visible, spoon the batter into the liners or cups. Overmixing muffins can make them less light.

Filling liners or cups
Unless otherwise stated, fill cupcake liners until they're almost full and the batter is level with the top of the liners. For muffins, the batter can extend above the tops of the cups slightly to achieve the "muffin top."

How to tell if a cake is baked
Cakes are usually slightly domed in the center with a lightly browned surface. Gently touch the surface with your flattened fingers; it should feel just firm. Some cakes require another test: pushing a toothpick into the center; if baked, it will come out clean.

Decorating techniques

Applying frostings and creams

Take a little of the frosting from the bowl using a small palette knife. Spread the frosting gently over each cake to cover it in an even layer before refining the application with the flat edge of the knife to level the surface.

Coloring ready-to-use fondant and marzipan (almond paste)

Using a toothpick, dot a little food coloring onto the fondant. If you want a delicate color, use a tiny amount because a little goes a long way. Working on a surface dusted with confectioners' sugar, knead in the color.

Covering cakes with ready-to-use fondant

Roll out the required amount of fondant thinly on a surface that is lightly dusted with confectioners' sugar to between 1/8 inch/3 mm and 1/4 inch/5 mm thick and 3 inches/7.5 cm in diameter. Lift over the cake and use your fingers to ease the fondant around the sides, pinching it together where there's a point. Cut off the excess at these points and tuck the fondant around the bottom before trimming off excess with a sharp knife.

Making a paper pastry bag

Cut out a 10-inch/25-cm square from parchment paper and fold it diagonally in half to make a triangle. Cut the paper in half on one side of the folded line to make two triangles. Holding one triangle with the long edge away from you, curl the right point over to meet the central point, forming a cone. Curl the left point over the cone. Adjust the points so there's no hole at the tip. Fold the points over to secure the cone in place.

Pastry bags and tips

Pastry bags can be fitted with tips or snipped at the tip. Fill the bag halfway with frosting and twist the open end together to seal. Snip off the tip and test the thickness of the piping, snipping off more, if necessary. (If using a piping tip, cut 1/2 inch/1.5 cm off the tip of the bag and fit with a tip before filling the bag and sealing it.) The tips used in this book are: a large star tip for lavish swirls; a small star tip for small stars or shells; and a writer tip for lines and dots.

Yellow cake

Makes: one 7-inch/18-cm
round or square cake
Prep: 15 minutes
Cook: 40 minutes

When using this moist, buttery yellow cake batter, follow the baking directions in your chosen recipe. To bake it as a yellow cake, put it in a 7-inch/ 18-cm round or square, greased and lined cake pan and bake for 40 minutes, or until firm to touch.

scant 1¾ cup lightly salted
butter, softened

¾ cup superfine sugar

1 tsp vanilla extract

3 eggs, beaten

heaping 1⅓ cups self-rising
flour

2 tbsp milk

1. Put the butter and sugar in a mixing bowl and beat them together with an electric handheld whisk until pale and fluffy. Beat in the vanilla. Add the eggs, a little at a time, beating between each addition. (If they are added too quickly, the batter will separate and the cake won't be as light.)

2. Sift in the flour, then stir it in gently with a metal spoon. As soon as the ingredients are combined, gently stir in the milk. The batter should drop easily from the spoon when tapped on the side of the bowl. (For a shortcut "all-in-one" method, put all the ingredients in the bowl together and beat until soft and creamy.) Bake as per your recipe or turn the batter out into a greased and lined 7-inch/18-cm cake pan and bake in an oven preheated to 350°F/180°C for 40 minutes.

Variations

White chocolate: Replace half of the sugar with 7 oz/200 g white chocolate, melted, stirring it into the batter after the eggs.

Lemon: Add the finely grated rind of 2 lemons when creaming the butter and sugar and use 2 tablespoons of lemon juice instead of vanilla and milk.

Orange: Add the finely grated rind of 1 orange when creaming the butter and sugar and use 2 tablespoons of orange juice instead of vanilla and milk.

Almond: Replace scant ½ cup flour with heaping ½ cup ground almonds and add 1 teaspoon of almond extract instead of the vanilla.

Buttercream

Makes: 1 quantity of
buttercream

Put scant ½ cup of unsalted butter in a mixing bowl and beat with an electric handheld whisk until softened. Add 1¼ cups of confectioners' sugar and beat with the whisk until smooth and creamy. Pour in 1 tablespoon of hot water and beat until soft and fluffy. For vanilla buttercream, beat in 1 teaspoon of vanilla extract with the confectioners' sugar. For lemon buttercream, beat in the finely grated rind of 1 lemon with the confectioners' sugar and use 2 tablespoons of lemon juice instead of the water.

Mini Classic Cakes

Carrot cakes

Makes: 20
Prep: 1 hour, plus cooling
Cook: 35 minutes

Carrot cake is such an all-time favorite that it simply had to be included here. If you're making these in advance, the little marzipan carrots can be positioned after frosting the cake, but don't add the leafy tops more than a few hours before serving, because they are likely to wilt.

scant ¾ cup lightly salted butter, softened, plus extra for greasing

¾ cup light brown sugar

3 eggs

scant 1¼ cups self-rising flour

½ tsp baking powder

½ tsp ground allspice

scant 1 cup ground almonds

finely grated rind of 1 lemon

1⅓ cups carrots, grated

½ cup coarsely chopped golden raisins

DECORATION

⅔ cup cream cheese

3 tbsp unsalted butter, softened

scant 1 cup confectioners' sugar, plus extra for dusting

2 tbsp lemon juice

2¼ oz/60 g marzipan

orange food coloring

several sprigs of dill

1. Preheat the oven to 350°F/180°C. Grease and line the bottom and sides of a 11-inch x 9-inch/28-cm x 23-cm baking pan. Grease the parchment paper. Put the butter, light brown sugar, eggs, flour, baking powder, allspice, almonds, and lemon rind in a mixing bowl and beat with an electric hand-held whisk until smooth and creamy. Stir in the carrots and raisins.

2. Turn the batter out into the pan and level the surface. Bake in the preheated oven for 35 minutes, or until risen and just firm to the touch. Let rest in the pan for 10 minutes, then transfer to a wire rack to cool.

3. For the decoration, beat together the cream cheese, butter, confectioners' sugar, and lemon juice until creamy. Color the marzipan deep orange (see page 8). Roll it into a sausage shape on a surface lightly dusted with confectioners' sugar, then divide it into 20 pieces and form each one into a small carrot shape, marking shallow grooves around each with a knife.

4. Using a palette knife, spread the frosting over the cake almost to the edges. Trim the crusts from the cake to neaten it, then cut it into 20 squares. Place a marzipan carrot on each cake and add a small sprig of dill.

Cherry and almond loaves

Makes: 12
Prep: 15 minutes, plus cooling
Cook: 20 minutes

Here is a bite-size mini treat for those who like traditional cakes. If you don't have a silicone loaf pan, use individual metal pans (see page 6) — because they are slightly larger, you'll have enough batter for only about 8 cakes, and these will need an extra 5 minutes' cooking time.

6 tbsp lightly salted butter, softened, plus extra for greasing

⅓ cup superfine sugar

1 egg

1 egg yolk

heaping ½ cup self-rising flour

½ tsp almond extract

heaping ½ cup ground almonds

¼ cup coarsely chopped natural candied cherries

2 tbsp slivered almonds

scant ½ cup confectioners' sugar

2 tsp lemon juice

1. Preheat the oven to 350°F/180°C. Place a 12-section silicone mini loaf pan on a baking sheet, or grease and line the bottom of individual mini loaf pans. Put the butter, superfine sugar, egg, egg yolk, flour, almond extract, and ground almonds in a mixing bowl and beat together with an electric handheld whisk until smooth and creamy. Stir in the cherries.

2. Using a teaspoon, spoon the batter into the pan sections and level with the back of the spoon. Break up the slivered almonds slightly by squeezing them in your hands and scatter them over the cake batter. Bake in the preheated oven for 20 minutes (25 minutes if using pans), or until risen and just firm to the touch. Let rest in the pan for 5 minutes, then transfer to a wire rack to cool.

3. Beat the confectioners' sugar and lemon juice together in a small bowl and drizzle over the cakes with a teaspoon. Let set.

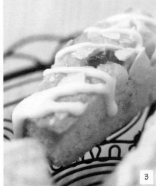

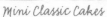

Mango cakes

Makes: 12

Prep: 15 minutes, plus cooling, plus 2–3 hours soaking

Cook: 20 minutes

½ cup finely chopped dried mango

finely grated rind of 1 orange, plus 3 tbsp juice

1 oz/25 g creamed coconut

6 tbsp lightly salted butter, softened, plus extra for greasing

⅓ cup superfine sugar

1 egg

⅔ cup self-rising flour

confectioners' sugar, for dusting

Dried mango and creamed coconut (available on the Internet) give these little cakes a fresh, tropical flavor, heightened by a hint of orange. They'll keep in an airtight container for several days.

1. Preheat the oven to 350°F/180°C. Place a 12-section silicone mini loaf pan on a baking sheet, or grease and line the bottom of individual mini loaf pans. Put the mango and orange juice in a small bowl and let stand, covered, for 2–3 hours, or until the orange juice is mostly absorbed. Finely grate the coconut (if it's firm and difficult to grate, first warm it briefly in the microwave).

2. Put the coconut, butter, sugar, egg, flour, and orange rind in a mixing bowl and beat together with an electric handheld whisk until smooth and pale. Stir in the mango and any unabsorbed orange juice.

3. Using a teaspoon, spoon the batter into the pan sections and level with the back of the spoon. Bake in the preheated oven for 20 minutes (25 minutes if using pans), or until risen and just firm to the touch. Let rest in the pan for 5 minutes, then transfer to a wire rack to cool.

4. Serve lightly dusted with confectioners' sugar.

Mini layer cakes

Makes: 12
Prep: 20 minutes, plus cooling
Cook: 15 minutes

So tiny and dainty, these "doll's house"-size cakes are just right with a cup of coffee when you don't want anything too rich or filling. Because of their size, they'll dry out quickly, so store them in an airtight container or freeze if making ahead.

5 tbsp lightly salted butter, softened, plus extra for greasing

⅓ cup superfine sugar

heaping ½ cup self-rising flour

1 egg

1 egg yolk

1 tsp vanilla extract

DECORATION

⅔ cup heavy cream

6 tbsp strawberry jelly

⅔ cup confectioners' sugar

1 tbsp lemon juice

1. Preheat the oven to 350°F/180°C. Place a 12-section silicone mini muffin pan on a baking sheet, or grease and line the bottom of a 12-section mini muffin pan. Put the butter, superfine sugar, flour, egg, egg yolk, and vanilla in a mixing bowl and beat together with an electric handheld whisk until it is smooth and creamy.

2. Using a teaspoon, spoon the batter into the pan sections and level with the back of the spoon. Bake in the preheated oven for 15 minutes, or until risen and just firm to the touch. Let stand in the pan for 5 minutes, then transfer to a wire rack to cool.

3. For the decoration, whip the cream until it just holds peaks. Split the cakes in half horizontally, using a small serrated knife. Set aside 2 tablespoons of the jelly, putting it in a small paper pastry bag and snipping off the tip (see page 8). Sandwich the cakes together with the remaining jelly and the cream.

4. Beat the confectioners' sugar and lemon juice together in a bowl until smooth. Spoon the icing over the cakes, spreading it to the edges. Pipe dots of jelly on each cake and draw a wooden toothpick through them.

Frosted baby bundt cakes

Makes: 12
Prep: 20 minutes, plus cooling
Cook: 15-20 minutes

1⅔ cup all-purpose flour,
plus extra for sprinkling

1 tsp baking powder

1 tsp ground cinnamon,
plus extra for sprinkling

⅔ cup superfine sugar

½ cup finely chopped walnuts

2 small baking apples, peeled,
cored, and finely grated

6 tbsp vegetable oil, plus extra
for greasing

3 eggs

⅔ cup buttermilk

FROSTING

3 tbsp plain yogurt

scant 1¼ cups confectioners'
sugar, sifted

This cake recipe is made with cinnamon, walnuts, and apples for a really moist texture. Don't be put off if you don't have mini Bundt pans; any small pans with a similar capacity can be used just as effectively instead.

1. Preheat the oven to 350°F/180°C. Brush 2 x 6-section mini Bundt pans with vegetable oil. Sprinkle a little flour into the pans and tilt so that both the bottoms and sides are coated; tap out the excess.

2. Sift the flour, baking powder, and cinnamon into a mixing bowl. Stir in the superfine sugar, walnuts, and apples.

3. In a separate mixing bowl, beat together the oil, eggs, and buttermilk. Add them to the dry ingredients and mix to form a soft paste.

4. Using a teaspoon, spoon the batter into the pans and level with the back of the spoon. Bake in the preheated oven for 15-20 minutes, or until risen and just firm to the touch. Let stand in the pans for 5 minutes, then transfer to a wire rack to cool.

5. For the frosting, put the yogurt into a bowl and add the confectioners' sugar. Beat together well until smooth. Spoon a little of the frosting onto the top of each cake, easing it slightly down the sides with the back of the spoon so the frosting runs down the flutes around the sides. Lightly sprinkle the tops of the cakes with cinnamon.

Coffee crumb cakes

Makes: 18
Prep: 30 minutes, plus cooling
Cook: 30–35 minutes

4 tbsp lightly salted butter,
softened, plus extra for greasing

½ cup superfine sugar

1 egg

5 tbsp sour cream

1 cup self-rising flour

TOPPING

⅔ cup all-purpose flour

5 tbsp lightly salted butter,
cut into pieces

½ tsp ground apple pie spice

1½ tsp ground espresso coffee

heaping ½ cup superfine sugar

ICING

⅔ cup confectioners' sugar

1 tbsp strong espresso coffee

One of these treats is an ideal accompaniment to a midmorning cup of coffee or tea. The crumb topping is sweet and streusel-like, in delicious contrast to the light and airy cake underneath it.

1. Preheat the oven to 350°F/180°C. Grease and line the bottom and sides of a shallow 7-inch/18-cm square, loose-bottom cake pan. Grease the parchment paper.

2. For the topping, put the all-purpose flour, butter, apple pie spice, and coffee in a food processor and blend until the mixture starts to resemble coarse breadcrumbs. Add the superfine sugar and blend again briefly. Turn the mixture into a mixing bowl.

3. For the batter, put the butter, superfine sugar, egg, sour cream, and self-rising flour in the food processor and blend until smooth and creamy, then turn out into the pan and level the surface. Sprinkle the crumb mixture in an even layer on top. Bake in the preheated oven for 30–35 minutes, or until risen and just firm to the touch and a toothpick inserted into the center comes out clean. Let stand in the pan for 10 minutes, then transfer to a wire rack to cool.

4. For the icing, put all but 2 tablespoons of the confectioners' sugar in a small mixing bowl and add the coffee. Beat to a smooth paste that falls in a thick trail from the spoon, adding a little more confectioners' sugar, if necessary. Cut the cake into 3 even pieces, then cut across to make 18 rectangular pieces. Drizzle with the icing.

gooey chocolate fudge bites

Makes: 21
Prep: 25 minutes, plus cooling
Cook: 35 minutes

This is as rich and delicious as chocolate cake can be! It's moist and gooey, with a generous amount of chocolate fudge frosting. Store in a cool place, not the refrigerator, so that the texture isn't ruined.

scant 1 cup lightly salted butter, cut into pieces, plus extra for greasing

7 oz/200 g semisweet chocolate, coarsely chopped

scant ½ cup heavy cream

3 eggs

¾ cup light brown sugar

heaping ¾ cup flour

FROSTING

7 oz/200 g semisweet chocolate

3 tbsp light corn syrup

4 tbsp unsalted butter, cut into pieces

heaping ½ cup confectioners' sugar, sifted

1. Preheat the oven to 325°F/160°C. Grease and line the bottom and sides of an 8-inch/20-cm square cake pan. Grease the parchment paper.

2. Put the butter, chocolate, and cream in a heatproof bowl, set the bowl over a saucepan of gently simmering water, and heat until melted. Let stand to cool slightly.

3. Put the eggs and light brown sugar in a mixing bowl and beat together with an electric handheld whisk until the batter begins to turn frothy. Stir in the cooled chocolate mixture. Sift in the flour and stir it in gently.

4. Turn the batter into the pan and level the surface. Bake in the preheated oven for 35 minutes, or until risen and just firm to the touch. Let stand in the pan for 10 minutes, then transfer to a wire rack to cool.

5. For the frosting, put 6 oz/175 g of the chocolate in a small heavy-bottom saucepan with the syrup and butter. Heat gently, stirring frequently, until the mixture is smooth and glossy. Transfer the mixture to a mixing bowl and beat in the confectioners' sugar. Let stand until the frosting has thickened enough to just hold its shape.

6. Split the cake in half horizontally and spread half of the fudge frosting on the cut side of the bottom piece. Place the other piece on top, cut-side down, and spread the remaining frosting on top of the cake. Using a sharp knife, carefully cut thin shards from the remaining chocolate. (If it's too brittle, heat briefly in the microwave and try again.) Trim off the edges of the cake to neaten it, then cut it into 21 rectangles. Scatter the shards on top.

Chocolate brownies

Makes: 25
Prep: 15 minutes, plus cooling
Cook: 18–20 minutes

These little brownies have the familiar sugary crust and soft gooey center that we've come to know and love. They're impossible to resist, so it's a good thing they're only bite-size!

½ cup lightly salted butter,
cut into pieces, plus extra
for greasing

3½ oz/100 g semisweet
chocolate, coarsely chopped

2 eggs

scant 1 cup light brown sugar

2 tsp vanilla extract

scant ½ cup all-purpose flour

¼ cup unsweetened cocoa

⅓ cup coarsely chopped pecans
or walnuts

1. Preheat the oven to 400°F/200°C. Grease and line the bottom and sides of a shallow 7-inch/18-cm square, loose-bottom cake pan.

2. Put the butter and chocolate in a heatproof bowl, set the bowl over a saucepan of gently simmering water, and heat until melted. Let the mixture stand to cool slightly.

3. Put the eggs, sugar, and vanilla in a mixing bowl and beat together with an electric handheld whisk until the batter begins to turn frothy. Stir in the chocolate mixture until combined.

4 Sift the flour and cocoa into the bowl and scatter in the nuts. Stir together gently, then turn the batter into the pan and level the surface.

5. Bake in the preheated oven for 18–20 minutes, or until the crust feels dry but gives a little when gently pressed. (If you're unsure, it's better to slightly undercook brownies because they lose their gooeyness when they are overbaked.) Let stand in the pan for 10 minutes, then transfer to a wire rack to cool. Cut the cake into 25 squares.

Vanilla swirl brownies

Makes: 12
Prep: 20 minutes, plus cooling
Cook: 12–15 minutes

6 tbsp lightly salted butter,
plus extra for greasing

3½ oz/100 g semisweet
chocolate, coarsely chopped

1 egg

1 egg yolk

½ cup light brown sugar

⅓ cup self-rising flour

¼ tsp baking powder

3 oz/85 g milk chocolate,
coarsely chopped

FROSTING

5½ oz/150 g mascarpone cheese

¼ cup confectioners' sugar

1 tsp vanilla extract

milk or semisweet chocolate
curls, to sprinkle

These rich, chocolatey morsels are great as an afternoon treat — and even better with coffee after a special dinner with friends.

1. Preheat the oven to 375°F/190°C. Grease and line the bottom of a 12-section mini muffin pan.

2. Put the butter and semisweet chocolate in a heatproof bowl, set the bowl over a saucepan of gently simmering water, and heat until melted. Let the mixture stand to cool slightly.

3. Put the egg, egg yolk, and light brown sugar in a mixing bowl and beat together with an electric handheld whisk until the batter begins to turn frothy. Stir in the melted chocolate. Sift the flour and baking powder into the bowl, scatter in the milk chocolate, and stir together. Using a teaspoon, spoon the batter into the pan sections.

4. Bake in the preheated oven for 12–15 minutes, or until the crust feels dry but gives a little when gently pressed. (If you're unsure, it's better to slightly undercook brownies because they lose their gooeyness when overbaked.) Let stand in the pan for 10 minutes, then transfer to a wire rack to cool.

5. For the frosting, put the mascarpone cheese, confectioners' sugar, and vanilla in a small bowl and beat with an electric handheld whisk until smooth and creamy. Put the mixture in a pastry bag fitted with a ½-inch/1-cm star tip and pipe swirls over the cakes. Sprinkle with chocolate curls.

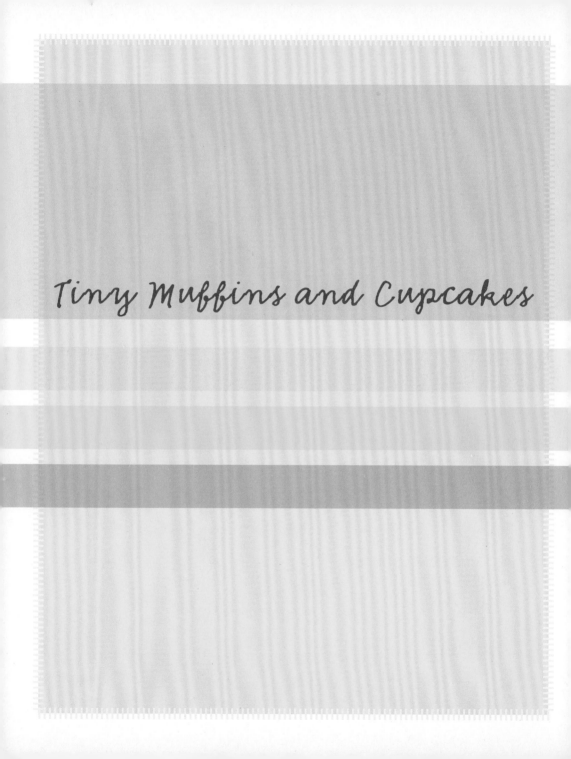

Tiny Muffins and Cupcakes

Blueberry and vanilla muffins

Makes: 18
Prep: 10 minutes, plus cooling
Cook: 15 minutes

In these fresh blueberry muffins, the plump, juicy fruits burst during baking to color and flavor the light, airy cake. This recipe uses homemade paper liners, made by pressing squares of parchment paper into the muffin pan.

1 cup self-rising flour

½ tsp baking powder

heaping ½ cup superfine sugar

heaping ½ cup blueberries

2 tsp vanilla extract

1 egg

½ cup buttermilk

2 tbsp vegetable oil

vanilla sugar, for dusting

1. Preheat the oven to 375°F/190°C. Cut out 18 x 3½-inch/9-cm squares from parchment paper. Push the squares into 2 x 12-section mini muffin pans, creasing the squares to fit so that they form paper liners. Don't worry if they lift out of the sections slightly; the weight of the muffin batter will hold them in place.

2. Sift the flour and baking powder into a mixing bowl. Stir in the sugar and blueberries. In a separate mixing bowl, beat together the vanilla, egg, buttermilk, and oil with a fork until evenly combined.

3. Turn the buttermilk mixture into the flour. Using a metal spoon, gently fold the ingredients together until only just mixed. (Don't overblend the ingredients or the muffins won't be as light.)

4. Spoon the batter into the paper liners; it should be level with the top of the pan. Sprinkle with a little vanilla sugar and bake in the preheated oven for 15 minutes, or until risen and just firm to the touch. Let the muffins stand in the pan for 2 minutes, then transfer them in their liners to a wire rack to cool. Serve warm or cold, dusted with extra vanilla sugar.

Cranberry muffins

Makes: 18
Prep: 10 minutes, plus cooling
Cook: 12–15 minutes

These muffins can be prepared and baked in less than half an hour, perfect for a relaxed weekend breakfast. For flavor variations, try adding the grated rind of an orange or a sprinkling of ground ginger or cinnamon.

heaping ¾ cup self-rising flour

½ tsp baking powder

¼ cup superfine sugar

¾ cup coarsely chopped dried cranberries

scant ½ cup plain yogurt

1 egg

2 tbsp vegetable oil

confectioners' sugar, for dusting

1. Preheat the oven to 375°F/190°C. Line 2 x 12-section mini muffin pans with 18 x 1¼-inch/3-cm mini paper liners.

2. Sift the flour and baking powder into a mixing bowl. Stir in the superfine sugar and cranberries. In a separate mixing bowl, beat together the yogurt, egg, and vegetable oil with a fork until evenly combined.

3. Turn the yogurt mixture into the flour. Using a metal spoon, gently fold the ingredients together until only just mixed. (Don't overblend the ingredients or the muffins won't be as light.)

4. Spoon the batter into the paper liners; it should be level with the top of the pan. Bake in the preheated oven for 12–15 minutes, or until risen and just firm to the touch. Let the muffins stand in the pan for 2 minutes, then transfer them in their liners to a wire rack to cool. Serve warm or cold, dusted with confectioners' sugar.

Double chocolate muffins

Makes: 12
Prep: 15 minutes, plus cooling
Cook: 15 minutes

Because these muffins are tiny, it's only right that they're as packed with chocolate as they could be! Any that are not eaten fresh from the oven can be kept for two days in an airtight container. Warm them for a few minutes in a moderate oven to revive their flavor.

2½ tbsp unsweetened cocoa

heaping ½ cup self-rising flour

¼ tsp baking powder

2 tbsp light brown sugar

3 oz/85 g coarsely chopped milk chocolate

1 egg

3 tbsp milk

3 tbsp lightly salted butter, melted

1½ oz/40 g semisweet chocolate, coarsely chopped

1. Preheat the oven to 375°F/190°C. Line a 12-section mini muffin pan with 1¼-inch/3-cm mini paper liners.

2. Sift the unsweetened cocoa, flour, and baking powder into a mixing bowl. Stir in the light brown sugar and milk chocolate. In a separate mixing bowl, beat together the egg, milk, and butter with a fork until evenly combined.

3. Turn the egg mixture into the flour. Using a metal spoon, gently fold the ingredients together until only just mixed. (Don't overblend the ingredients or the muffins won't be as light.)

4. Spoon the batter into the paper liners; it should be level with the top of the pan. Bake in the preheated oven for 15 minutes, or until risen and just firm to the touch. Let the muffins stand in the pan for 2 minutes, then transfer them in their liners to a wire rack to cool.

5. Put the semisweet chocolate in a heatproof bowl, set over a saucepan of gently simmering water, and heat until melted. Using a teaspoon, drizzle the melted chocolate over the muffins and serve warm or cold.

Maple and banana cupcakes

Makes: 12
Prep: 20 minutes, plus cooling
Cook: 18–20 minutes

Banana cake invariably appeals to everyone, from tiny tots to adults. These mini ones can be served plain, simply dusted with confectioners' sugar, or swirled with the delicious maple buttercream.

1 small banana

2 tbsp maple syrup

2 tbsp milk

4½ tbsp lightly salted butter, softened

heaping ½ cup superfine sugar

1 egg, beaten

heaping ¾ cup self-rising flour

FROSTING

scant ¾ cup lightly salted butter, softened

1 tsp vanilla extract

⅓ cup confectioners' sugar

scant ½ cup maple syrup

8 pecan or walnut halves, coarsely chopped, to decorate

1. Preheat the oven to 350°F/180°C. Line a 12-section mini muffin pan with 1¼-inch/3-cm mini paper liners.

2. In a small mixing bowl, mash the banana to a puree with a fork. Stir in the maple syrup and milk.

3. Put the butter and superfine sugar in a separate mixing bowl and beat together with an electric handheld whisk until light and fluffy. Gradually beat in the egg, a little at a time, adding a teaspoon of the flour if the mixture starts to separate.

4. Sift half of the flour into the bowl with the butter mixture, then add half of the banana. Gently fold the ingredients together until only just mixed. Sift in the remaining flour, add the remaining banana mixture, and fold in.

5. Spoon the batter into the paper liners. Bake in the preheated oven for 18–20 minutes, or until risen and just firm to the touch. Let stand in the pan for 5 minutes, then transfer to a wire rack to cool.

6. For the frosting, put the butter, vanilla, confectioners' sugar, and maple syrup in a bowl and beat with an electric handheld whisk until smooth and creamy. Put the frosting in a small paper pastry bag fitted with a ½-inch/1-cm star tip and use to decorate the cupcakes. Scatter with nuts.

Almond daisy cupcakes

Makes: 12
Prep: 25 minutes, plus cooling
Cook: 12–15 minutes

3 egg whites

⅓ cup all-purpose flour

⅔ cup confectioners' sugar

¾ cup ground almonds

5 tbsp lightly salted butter, melted and cooled

DECORATION

1 quantity Lemon Buttercream (see page 9)

red, black, and lime green food colorings

heaping ⅓ cup whole blanched almonds

6 red and 6 black mini jelly beans

These fun flower cupcakes will add a welcome splash of springtime color to the table. The buttercream topping is fresh and lemony, while the almond cake is moist, nutty, and light.

1. Preheat the oven to 400°F/200°C. Line a 12-section mini muffin pan with 1¼-inch/3-cm mini paper liners, preferably in red or black.

2. Whisk the eggs whites in a clean mixing bowl until they're broken up but not fluffy. Add the flour, sugar, ground almonds, and butter and stir together to make a smooth paste. Spoon the batter into the paper liners. Bake in the preheated oven for 12–15 minutes, or until risen and just firm to the touch. Let stand in the pan for 5 minutes, then transfer to a wire rack.

3. For the decoration, spoon 2 tablespoons of the buttercream into a small bowl and color with red food coloring. Spoon an additional 2 tablespoons into another bowl and color black. Color the remaining buttercream lime green, and spread this over the cakes with a palette knife.

4. Using a sharp knife, carefully cut each blanched almond in half to make flat petal shapes. Press a jelly bean into the center of each cake and surround with almonds, pressing them gently into the buttercream to shape flowers.

5. Put the red buttercream in a small paper pastry bag and the black in another, and snip off the tips (see page 8). Pipe an outline around the edges of each almond, half in red and half in black.

Baby shower cupcakes

Makes: 18
Prep: 45 minutes, plus cooling
Cook: 15 minutes

5 tbsp lightly salted butter,
softened

....

heaping ½ cup superfine sugar

....

1 egg

....

1 egg yolk

....

heaping ½ cup self-rising flour

....

1 tsp vanilla extract

....

DECORATION

....

1 quantity Buttercream
(see page 9)

....

pink and blue food colorings

....

2 oz/55 g ready-to-use fondant

....

confectioners' sugar, for dusting

....

*These are so simple to make, but very pretty — and
perfect for the next baby shower. Pink and blue
look effective together, but you can change the
colors to any other combination.*

1. Preheat the oven to 350°F/180°C. Line 2 x 12-section mini muffin
pans with 18 x 1¼-inch/3-cm mini paper liners, preferably in deep
pink or blue.

2. Put the butter, superfine sugar, egg, egg yolk, flour, and vanilla
in a mixing bowl and beat together with an electric handheld whisk until
smooth and creamy. Spoon the mixture into the paper liners. Bake in the
preheated oven for 15 minutes, or until risen and just firm to the touch.
Let stand in the pans for 5 minutes, then transfer to a wire rack to cool.

3. For the decoration, divide the buttercream equally between 2 bowls
and color 1 with pink coloring and the other with blue, so they're pale
pastel. Using a palette knife, spread a thin layer of pink frosting over half
of the cakes and blue over the other half, reserving some for decoration.

4. Color the remaining buttercream in the bowls to a deeper tone and put
it in small paper pastry bags fitted with ½-inch/1-cm star tips. Pipe pink
shells around the blue cakes and blue shells around the pink ones.

5. Color half the ready-to-use fondant blue (see page 8) and wrap it tightly
in plastic wrap. Color the remainder pink and roll it out thinly on a surface
lightly dusted with confectioners' sugar.

6. Cut the pink fondant into ½-inch/1-cm-wide strips, then cut across these
at 1-inch/2.5-cm intervals to make tiny rectangles. Use 2 rectangles to shape
bow ends, pinching the ends together as you position them on the blue-
edge cakes. Bend 2 more rectangles into loops, pinching the ends together,
and secure with a damp paintbrush to complete each bow. Use the blue
fondant in the same way to make bows for the pink-edge cakes.

Chocolate and raspberry cupcakes

Makes: 20
Prep: 50 minutes, plus cooling
Cook: 12–15 minutes

heaping ½ cup raspberries

heaping ½ cup unsweetened cocoa

scant ½ cup boiling water

4 tbsp lightly salted butter, softened

⅔ cup light brown sugar

1 egg, beaten

heaping ¾ cup self-rising flour

DECORATION

3 tbsp lightly salted butter

3½ oz/100 g semisweet chocolate, coarsely chopped

2 tbsp light corn syrup

⅓ cup raspberries

⅔ cup confectioners' sugar, sifted

Here's your chance to get carried away with special messages on these pretty cakes — hearts, kisses, whatever you desire! Once decorated, they'll keep fresh for a couple of days in a cool place.

1. Preheat the oven to 350°F/180°C. Line 2 x 12-section mini muffin pans with 20 x 1¼-inch/3-cm mini paper liners, preferably in deep pink or brown.

2. Put the raspberries in a small mixing bowl and crush with a fork until they are broken up. In a separate mixing bowl, whisk the unsweetened cocoa with the boiling water. Let stand to cool.

3. Put the butter and light brown sugar in a third mixing bowl and beat together with an electric handheld whisk until light and fluffy. Beat in the egg a little at a time.

4. Stir in the flour and the cocoa mixture until evenly combined, then add the raspberries and mix together lightly. Spoon the batter into the paper liners. Bake in the preheated oven for 12–15 minutes, or until risen and just firm to the touch. Let stand in the pans for 5 minutes, then transfer to a wire rack to cool.

5. For the decoration, melt the butter in a small saucepan and add the chocolate and syrup. Heat very gently until the chocolate has almost melted, then turn into a mixing bowl. Let stand to cool, stirring frequently, until the mixture has thickened enough to almost hold its shape. Spoon it over the cakes and spread to the edges using a palette knife.

6. Crush the raspberries and press them through a strainer, using the back of a spoon to extract the juice. Sift the confectioners' sugar over the juice and stir to make a loose paste. Put the icing in a small paper pastry bag and snip off the tip (see page 8). Pipe hearts and kisses onto the cakes.

Red velvet heart cupcakes

Makes: 12
Prep: 1–1½ hours, plus cooling
Cook: 15 minutes

1 small raw beet, finely grated

1 egg

2 tbsp buttermilk or sour cream

1 tsp vinegar

4 tbsp lightly salted butter,
softened

¼ cup light brown sugar

⅔ cup self-rising flour

2 tsp unsweetened cocoa

DECORATION

½ quantity Buttercream
(see page 9)

2½ oz/70 g ready-to-use fondant

deep red food coloring

confectioners' sugar, for dusting

These cakes take a little while to decorate, but the results will certainly be worth the effort. Make yourself comfortable and enjoy!

1. Preheat the oven to 350°F/180°C. Line a 12-section mini muffin pan with 1¼-inch/3-cm mini paper liners in deep red or white.

2. Put the beet, egg, buttermilk, and vinegar in a mixing bowl and stir together until well combined. Put the butter and light brown sugar in a separate mixing bowl and beat together with an electric handheld whisk until pale and fluffy. Sift half of the flour and unsweetened cocoa into the butter mixture and turn in the beet mixture. Stir gently until evenly combined. Sift in the remaining flour and cocoa and stir again to mix.

3. Spoon the batter into the paper liners. Bake in the preheated oven for 15 minutes, or until risen and just firm to the touch. Let stand in the pan for 5 minutes, then transfer to a wire rack to cool.

4. For the decoration, spread the buttercream over the cakes using a palette knife. Color the ready-to-use fondant a deep red (see page 8).

5. Divide the fondant into 12 even pieces. Roll a piece of fondant into a thin rope 4½ inches/12 cm long. On a surface lightly dusted with confectioners' sugar, flatten it with a rolling pin, keeping it no more than ½-inch/1-cm wide. Cut it in half lengthwise, then across into 1-inch/2.5-cm pieces. Repeat with the remaining fondant. Roll each little piece up between your thumb and finger to resemble a tiny rose. Use the roses to build heart shapes on top of all the cakes by pressing them gently down into the buttercream.

Petite Party Cakes

Summer flower cakes

Makes: 16
Prep: 2½ hours, plus cooling
Cook: 25 minutes

These little cakes are a labor of love, but they look simply stunning. If you've planned a color theme for a special party, you can alter the colors of the vertical stripes to enhance it. Once decorated, they'll keep in a cool place for several days.

a little lightly salted butter,
for greasing

1 quantity Lemon Cake batter
(see page 9)

1 quantity Lemon Buttercream
(see page 9)

2 lb/900 g white ready-to-use
fondant

pink and purple food colorings

confectioners' sugar, for dusting

1. Preheat the oven to 350°F/180°C. Grease and line the bottom of a cake pan containing 16 x 2-inch/5-cm sections.

2. Put 2 teaspoons of the cake batter into each pan section. Bake in the preheated oven for 25 minutes, or until risen and just firm to the touch. Let stand in the pan for 5 minutes before carefully loosening each cake by running a slender knife around the sides of each section. Transfer the cakes to a wire rack to cool before peeling away the lining paper.

3. Reserve 3 tablespoons of the buttercream and use the remainder to spread a thin layer over the tops and sides of the cakes.

4. Reserve one-third of the ready-to-use fondant. From the remainder, color one-third pale pink, one-third purple, and one-third a darker pink (see page 8). Take half of each colored fondant and roll it out thinly on a surface lightly dusted with confectioners' sugar. Cut a strip from each color that is the depth of the cakes. Cut this into ¼-inch/5-mm-wide strips the depth of the cake and secure them, in alternating colors, around the sides of the cakes, pressing them gently into the buttercream. Use the remaining colored fondant to cover all the cakes.

5. Roll out the reserved white ready-to-use fondant as thinly as possible on a surface lightly dusted with confectioners' sugar and cut out simple flower shapes, using a ½-inch/15-mm plunger cutter. Press each cut flower shape out onto your finger and then place it on a cake. Repeat until you've built up a cluster of flowers on one cake, then repeat for all the cakes.

6. Color the reserved buttercream pink. Put it in a small paper pastry bag and snip off the tip (see page 8). Pipe little dots in the centers of all the white flowers.

White party stars

Makes: 9–10
Prep: 1–1½ hours, plus cooling
Cook: 25–30 minutes

These pretty little stars would make a great addition to a special occasion; you could substitute the color of your choice to tie in with your party theme.

unsalted butter, for greasing

1 quantity Orange Cake batter (see page 9)

1 quantity Orange Buttercream (see page 9)

14 oz/400 g white ready-to-use fondant

1 egg white

1⅔ cups confectioners' sugar, sifted, plus extra for dusting

lilac food coloring

1. Preheat the oven to 350°F/180°C. Grease and line the bottom and sides of a 11-inch x 9-inch/26-cm x 22-cm baking pan.

2. Turn the cake batter into the pan and level the surface. Bake in the preheated oven for 25–30 minutes, or until risen and just firm to the touch. Let stand in the pan for 10 minutes, then transfer to a wire rack to cool.

3. If the cake has risen in the center, cut off a thin slice with a large knife. Using a 3-inch/7.5-cm star cutter as a guide, cut out shapes from the cake. (Cut each star shape as close to the previously cut star as possible so you don't waste any cake; freeze the cake trimmings for making Mini Cake Pops, see page 68, another time.) Turn the cakes over so that the bottom forms a flat top.

4. Using a palette knife, spread a thin layer of buttercream over the top and sides of each star.

5. Divide the ready-to-use fondant into 9–10 equal pieces (depending on the number of stars you cut from the cake). Roll out a piece of the fondant on a surface lightly dusted with confectioners' sugar to a circle about 4½ inches/11 cm in diameter. Lift it over a star cake and fit the sides, pinching the fondant together at the points. Cut off the excess at the points and then cut around the bottom of the cake. Repeat with the remaining cakes.

6. Beat the egg white in a clean bowl with the half of the confectioners' sugar until smooth. Gradually work in the remaining confectioners' sugar until softly forming peaks. Add a little lilac food coloring and put the icing in a small paper pastry bag fitted with a little writer tip (see page 8). Pipe tiny dots in the center of the tops of the cakes.

Birthday balloons

Makes: 24
Prep: 1–1½ hours, plus cooling
Cook: 18–20 minutes

1 quantity White Chocolate Cake
batter (see page 9)

2 quantities Buttercream
(see page 9)

12 oz/350 g smally chewy taffy-
style candies in 3 different
flavors, such as strawberry,
orange, and lemon

24 x 2½-inch/6-cm lollipop sticks

3½ oz/100 g small red, green,
and yellow sugar-coated
chocolate candies

*Kids will love these fun, colorful cakes, lavishly
decorated with tempting treats. Use candles
to replace some of the balloons if you prefer.*

1. Preheat the oven to 350°F/180°C. Line 2 x 12-section mini muffin pans
with 1½-inch/4-cm mini paper liners, preferably in pink, green, or yellow.

2. Spoon the cake batter into the paper liners. Bake in the preheated oven
for 18–20 minutes, until risen and just firm to the touch. Let stand in the
pan for 5 minutes, then transfer to a wire rack to cool.

3. Using a palette knife, spread a thin layer of buttercream over the cakes.

4. For each balloon, take about 2 of the chewy candies of the same color
and mold them into a ball. (If they are brittle or too firm to shape, first
microwave them on medium power for 5–6 seconds to soften them. Don't
overheat them or they'll turn to a molten syrup.) Push each balloon shape
onto the end of a lollipop stick. Pinch the candy around the stick to create
the effect of a knotted end. Repeat until you have enough balloons, pushing
each into a cake.

5. For the streamers, soften the remaining chewy candies as above and
roll them out thinly. Cut them into 2-inch x ¼-inch/5-cm x 5-mm pieces
and curl each one around a lollipop stick. Twist the candies off the sticks
and arrange them on the cakes. Scatter with the sugar-coated candies
to finish.

Mini party cakes

Makes: 16
Prep: 1¼ hours, plus cooling
Cook: 40 minutes

A platter of these delicious cakes will look impressive at any special get-together. Make them a couple of days in advance, so you've got time to enjoy the decorating before more pressing party tasks arise. For a big birthday, use number sparklers, too.

a little lightly salted butter, for greasing

1 quantity Yellow Cake batter (see page 9)

1 quantity Vanilla Buttercream (see page 9)

heart-shape sugar sprinkles

pearl balls

1. Preheat the oven to 350°F/180°C. Grease and line the bottom and sides of a 7-inch/18-cm square cake pan.

2. Spoon the cake batter into the pan and level the surface with the back of the spoon. Bake in the preheated oven for 40 minutes, or until risen and just firm to the touch. Let stand in the pan for 10 minutes, then transfer to a wire rack to cool.

3. Cut a ½-inch/1-cm crust off the edges of the cake, then cut the cake into 16 even squares.

4. Put the buttercream in a paper pastry bag fitted with a small star tip (see page 8). Place the cakes in paper cake liners.

5. Pipe vertical lines down the sides and over the top edges of the cakes. Scatter the tops of the cakes with sugar sprinkles and pearl balls.

Pupcakes

Makes: 12
Prep: 1½ hours, plus cooling
Cook: 15 minutes

5 tbsp lightly salted butter,
softened, plus extra for greasing

¼ cup superfine sugar

heaping ½ cup self-rising flour

1 egg

1 egg yolk

1 tsp vanilla extract

1 oz/25 g white chocolate,
finely chopped

DECORATION

heaping 2⅓ cups confectioners'
sugar

3 tbsp cold water

blue and black food colorings

16 white chewy taffy-style
candies

8 black chewy taffy-style candies

½ quantity Buttercream
(see page 9)

small piece pink chewy taffy-
style candy

small piece yellow chewy taffy-
style candy

Chewy taffy-style candies are great for shaping and modeling cake decorations. These cute little puppy faces will provide plenty of fun at a kids' party or special meal — the kids can help you make them!

1. Preheat the oven to 350°F/180°C. Place a 12-section silicone mini muffin pan on a baking sheet, or grease and line the bottom of a 12-section mini muffin pan. Put the butter, superfine sugar, flour, egg, egg yolk, and vanilla in a mixing bowl and beat together with an electric handheld whisk until smooth and creamy. Stir in the chocolate.

2. Using a teaspoon, spoon the mixture into the pan sections and level with the back of the spoon. Bake in the preheated oven for 15 minutes, or until risen and just firm to the touch. Let stand on the baking sheet for 5 minutes, then transfer to a wire rack to cool.

3. For the decoration, put the confectioners' sugar in a bowl and beat in 2 tablespoons of the water. Add the third tablespoon gradually, stirring with a wooden spoon until the icing is smooth and slowly drips off the back of the spoon. Stir in a little blue food coloring.

4. Dip a cake into the icing until coated. Lift the cake out of the bowl on a fork and let the excess icing drip back into the bowl before transferring the cake to the wire rack. Repeat with the remaining cakes.

5. Using a rolling pin, flatten the white chewy candies one at a time. (If they are brittle or too firm to shape, first microwave them on medium power for 5–6 seconds to soften them. Don't overheat them or they'll turn into a molten syrup.) Using scissors, cut out rounds from the white candies, about 1½ inches/4 cm in diameter, and secure them to the tops of the cakes with a little water.

6. Roll pea-size balls of the black chewy candies into long, flat "ears" (first softening the candies as above if brittle) and position them on the cakes. Use smaller pieces for noses.

7. Beat a little black food coloring into the buttercream. Put it in a paper pastry bag and snip off the tip (see page 8). Use to pipe eyes, a mouth, and whiskers onto each face. Use the pink chewy candies to shape tongues and yellow chewy candies to shape collars. If liked, shape small bones from the leftover white candies and rest them next to the cakes.

Halloween cakes

Makes: 18
Prep: 1½ hours, plus cooling
Cook: 40 minutes

a little lightly salted butter,
for greasing

2 quantities Orange Cake batter
(see page 9)

2 tbsp lemon juice

2 tbsp orange juice

3 tbsp honey

6 tbsp apricot preserve or jam

2 tbsp hot water

orange food coloring

1 lb 10 oz/750 g white ready-to-
use fondant

confectioners' sugar, for dusting

2 oz/55 g coarsely chopped
semisweet chocolate

several soft green jelly candies

20 small Oreo cookies, filling
removed

*Serve these cakes at a Halloween party, or box them
up for impressive "take home" gifts. They look
particularly stunning on a dark plate or cloth.*

1. Preheat the oven to 350°F/180°C. Grease and line the bottom and
sides of a 10½-inch x 8½-inch/26-cm x 22-cm baking pan. Grease the
parchment paper.

2. Turn the cake batter into the pan and level the surface. Bake in the
preheated oven for 40 minutes, or until risen and just firm to the touch.
Let stand in the pan for 10 minutes, then transfer to a wire rack to cool.

3. If the cake has risen in the center, cut off a thin slice with a large knife.
Using a 2½-inch/6-cm half-moon cutter as a guide, cut out shapes from
the cake. Turn the cakes over so that the bottom forms a flat top.

4. Mix the juices with the honey in a small pitcher and drizzle over the
surface of the cakes so the syrup seeps into them. Press the preserve
through a small strainer into a bowl and stir in the hot water. Brush this
mixture over the tops and sides of the cakes.

5. Knead orange food coloring into the ready-to-use fondant (see page 8).
Divide the fondant into 18 equal pieces. Roll out a piece of fondant on
a surface lightly dusted with confectioners' sugar to an oval 6 inches x
4 inches/15 cm x 10 cm. Lift it over a half-moon cake and fit it around the
sides, pinching the fondant together at the points. Cut off the excess at
these points and then cut around the bottom of the cake. Repeat with the
remaining cakes, reserving the fondant trimmings.

6. Put the chocolate in a heatproof bowl, set the bowl over a saucepan
of gently simmering water, and heat until melted. Put the chocolate
in a small paper pastry bag and snip off the tip (see page 8). Color the
fondant trimmings a deeper orange and shape them into small balls. Mark
"pumpkin" ridges with the back of a knife. Cut small pieces of soft jelly
candies and push them into the tops for stalks, securing with chocolate.

7. To shape bats, heat an Oreo cookie in the microwave until it's soft
(this will take 1½–2 minutes, but check after a minute). Cut a circle from
one side with a 1-inch/2.5-cm cutter. Cut small flutes from the opposite
sides with a ½-inch/1.5-cm cutter. Secure the decorations in place with
chocolate and pipe bat eyes and extra bats around the sides of the cakes.

Party presents

Makes: 16
Prep: 1½ hours, plus cooling and decorating
Cook: 45 minutes

a little lightly salted butter, for greasing

1 quantity White Chocolate or Almond Cake batter (see page 9)

1 quantity Buttercream (see page 9)

½ cup apricot preserve or jam

2 tbsp brandy, almond or orange liqueur, or water

1 lb 14 oz/850 g white marzipan

green, blue, and pink food colorings

confectioners' sugar, for dusting

2 oz/55 g coarsely chopped white chocolate

3 yd/3 m deep pink ribbon, about ½-inch/1-cm wide

3 yd/3 m yellow ribbon, about ¼-inch/5-mm wide

Marzipan makes a wonderful cake covering, particularly for those who find the sweetness of fondant too much. It can be colored, rolled, cut out, and shaped just as you would ready-to-use fondant, and it is equally fun to work with.

1. Preheat the oven to 350°F/180°C. Grease and line the bottom and sides of a 7-inch/18-cm square cake pan. Turn the cake batter out into the pan and level the surface. Bake in the preheated oven for 45 minutes, or until risen and just firm to the touch. Let stand in the pan for 10 minutes, then transfer to a wire rack to cool.

2. If the cake has risen in the center, cut off a thin slice with a large knife so that the surface of the cake is level. Split the cake in half horizontally and sandwich the halves together with the buttercream. Cut a ¼-inch/5-mm crust off the sides. Turn the cake over and check that it's completely level. Cut the cake into 16 even squares.

3. Press the preserve through a small strainer into a little saucepan and stir in the brandy. Heat gently until smooth. Color 1 oz/25 g of the marzipan green (see page 8) and another 1 oz/25 g blue and reserve both, wrapped separately in plastic wrap. Color the remaining marzipan pale pink. Brush the apricot glaze all over the tops and sides of the cake squares.

4. Divide the pink marzipan into 16 even pieces. Roll out a piece of the pink marzipan thinly on a surface lightly dusted with confectioners' sugar, to a 4½-inch/12-cm square. Lift it over a cake and fit it down the sides, pinching the excess together at the corners. Cut off the excess at these corners and then cut around the bottom of the cake. Repeat with the remaining cakes, reserving the marzipan trimmings.

5. Color the marzipan trimmings a deeper shade of pink and use, with the other colored marzipans, to shape simple gifts. Arrange on the cakes.

6. Put the chocolate in a heatproof bowl, set the bowl over a saucepan of gently simmering water, and heat until melted. Put the melted chocolate in a small paper pasry bag and snip off the tip (see page 8). Pipe lines over the gifts and around the top edges of the cakes. Cut the pink ribbon into 7½-inch/19-cm lengths and secure around the bottom of the cakes with dots of chocolate from the pastry bag. Cut the yellow ribbon into the same lengths and place these so they sit in the center of the pink ribbon, again secured with dots of the chocolate.

Mini ivory wedding cakes

Makes: 16
Prep: 1½ hours, plus cooling
Cook: 1 hour

Make these pretty cakes for a girls' night before the big day, or, of course, for the wedding party itself. Bake the cakes a day before decorating so they have time to firm up a little. Assemble the cakes a day before the party.

a little lightly salted butter, for greasing

2 quantities White Chocolate Cake batter (see page 9)

9 oz/250 g white ready-to-use fondant

brown or ivory food coloring

confectioners' sugar, for dusting

16 round, silver cake boards, about 3 inches/7.5 cm in diameter

1¼ cups heavy cream

10½ oz/300 g white chocolate, coarsely chopped

10 yd/10 m wired organza ribbon, about 1 inch/2.5 cm wide

1. Preheat the oven to 350°F/180°C. Grease and line the bottom and sides of a 9-inch/23-cm square cake pan.

2. Spoon two-thirds of the cake batter into the pan and level the surface with the back of the spoon. Bake in the preheated oven for 35 minutes, or until well risen and just firm to the touch. Let stand in the pan for 10 minutes, then transfer to a wire rack to cool. Wash and reline the pan and bake the remaining batter for 20–25 minutes, as before.

3. Color the ready-to-use fondant with a dash of brown food coloring (see page 8). Roll out half of the fondant as thinly as possible on a surface lightly dusted with confectioners' sugar. Cut out 8 rounds using a 3-inch/7.5-cm cookie cutter, rerolling the trimmings to make sufficient. Repeat with the other half. Dampen the surfaces of the cake boards and position a circle of fondant on each.

4. To make a ganache, heat half of the cream in a small saucepan until very hot but not boiling. Pour it into a mixing bowl and add the chocolate. Let stand, stirring frequently, until the chocolate has melted. Let cool completely. Stir in the remaining cream and beat very lightly with an electric handheld whisk on slow speed until the ganache is just thick enough to hold its shape. (If overmixed, the mixture might separate.)

5. Using a 2-inch/5-cm round cookie cutter as a guide, cut out 16 rounds from the deeper cake. Use a 1½-inch/4-cm round cutter as a guide to cut out 16 rounds from the shallower cake. (Freeze the trimmings for making trifle or Mini Cake Pops, see page 68, another time.) Place the larger cakes on the boards with the fondant, securing with a little ganache. Spread some of the remaining ganache over the tops and sides of these cakes with a palette knife. Position the smaller cakes on top and cover these with ganache in the same way. Let set in a cool place for 1–2 hours.

6. Cut the ribbon into 24-inch/60-cm lengths and wrap a length around each cake, securing at the tops with bows and cutting off any long ends.

Little Fabulous Cakes

Mini cake pops

Makes: 24
Prep: 1–1¼ hours, plus setting
Cook: 40 minutes

1 quantity Yellow or Almond
Cake, baked (see page 9),
or 1 lb/450 g store-bought
yellow cake

3 oz/85 g mascarpone cheese

heaping ½ cup confectioners'
sugar

½ tsp vanilla or almond
extract

DECORATION

8 oz/225 g milk chocolate,
coarsely chopped

24 lollipop sticks

scant 1¼ cups confectioners'
sugar

pink food coloring

4 tsp cold water

24 small candies, such as
miniature sugar-coated
chocolate candies

sugar sprinkles

*These mini "cupcake" cake pops have both child
and adult appeal, so they're ideal for a gathering
of mixed ages. Once iced, they'll keep in a cool
place for a couple of days.*

1. Line a baking sheet with parchment paper. Crumble the yellow cake into a mixing bowl. Add the mascarpone, confectioners' sugar, and vanilla and mix together until you have a thick paste.

2. Divide the paste into 24 even pieces. Roll one piece of the paste into a ball. Push this ball into a mini paper liner, pressing it down so that when it is removed from the liner you have a mini cupcake shape. Shape the remaining 23 cake pops in the same way. Place on the baking sheet and chill for 1–2 hours to firm up.

3. Put the chocolate in a heatproof bowl, set the bowl over a saucepan of gently simmering water, and heat until melted. Remove from the heat. Push a lollipop stick into each cake pop. Dip a cake pop into the chocolate, turning it until coated. Lift it from the bowl, letting the excess drip back into the bowl, then place it in a cup or glass. Repeat with the remaining cake pops. Chill or let stand in a cool place until the chocolate has set.

4. Put the confectioners' sugar in a mixing bowl and beat in a dash of pink food coloring and the water until smooth. The icing should almost hold its shape. Spoon a little onto a cake pop, easing it slightly down the sides with the side of a teaspoon. If the icing is too firm, you might need to add a dash more water. Before the icing sets, place a small candy in the center of each cake pop and scatter with sugar sprinkles.

Snowman cake pops

Makes: 20
Prep: 1¼ –1½ hours, plus setting

7 oz/200 g store-bought angel
food cake

heaping 2⅓ cups
confectioners' sugar

4 tbsp heavy cream

2 tsp peppermint extract

DECORATION

heaping 2⅓ cups
confectioners' sugar,
plus extra for piping

3 tbsp cold water

20 lollipop sticks

black, orange, red, and yellow
food colorings

3½ oz/100 g marzipan

Whether it's a winter birthday, Christmas, or New Year, these fun seasonal cake pops are perfect — especially if there's snow on the ground!

1. Line a baking sheet with parchment paper. Crumble the angel food cake into a mixing bowl. Add the confectioners' sugar, cream, and peppermint extract and mix together until you have a thick paste, adding a dash more cream if the mixture feels too dry.

2. Set aside one-quarter of the paste, then divide the remaining paste into 20 even balls to form the bottom of the snowmen. Now roll 20 balls from the reserved paste. Press a small ball onto a larger one to shape a snowman, and repeat for the remaining snowmen. Place on the baking sheet and chill for 1–2 hours to firm up.

3. Put the confectioners' sugar in a mixing bowl and beat in the water to make a paste that coats the back of a spoon in a thin layer. Push a lollipop stick or ice-cream stick through each snowman so it goes halfway into the smaller ball (or use bamboo skewers, or even chopsticks).

4. Dip a snowman in the icing, turning it until coated. Lift it from the bowl, letting the excess drip back into the bowl, then place it in a cup or glass. Repeat with the remaining snowmen, reserving some icing.

5. Beat a dash of black food coloring and a little extra confectioners' sugar into the icing left in the bowl so the mixture is thick enough to hold its shape. Put the icing in a small paper pastry bag and snip off the tip (see page 8).

6. Color a cherry-size ball of marzipan orange (see page 8), then half of the remaining marzipan red and the other half yellow. Use the red and yellow marzipan to shape tiny hats and scarves, pressing them into the fondant to secure. Shape and secure pointed noses in orange marzipan. Pipe eyes, mouths, and buttons using the black icing.

Chocolate mint cake pops

Makes: 26–28

Prep: 1 hour, plus setting

Cook: 5 minutes

10½ oz/300 g semisweet
chocolate, coarsely chopped

2 tbsp unsalted butter,
softened

1¾ oz/50 g hard mint candies

1 lb/450 g milk chocolate

1 cup coarsely chopped mini
marshmallows

26–28 x 2½-inch/6-cm
lollipop sticks

chocolate sprinkles,
to decorate

*This cake pop version of "rocky road" is as easy
to make as it gets! The milk chocolate coating has
family appeal, but you can use semisweet chocolate
instead for a more adult flavor.*

1. Line a baking sheet with parchment paper. Put the semisweet chocolate
in a heatproof bowl, set the bowl over a saucepan of gently simmering
water, and heat until melted. Stir in the butter. Let stand until the mixture
is cool but not beginning to set.

2. Put the mint candies in a plastic bag and tap firmly with a rolling
pin until they are broken into tiny pieces. Finely chop 5½ oz/150 g of
the milk chocolate, then stir it into the melted semisweet chocolate with
the mints and marshmallows until thoroughly mixed.

3. As soon as the mixture is firm enough to hold its shape, divide and roll
into 26–28 even balls. Place the balls on the baking sheet and chill in the
refrigerator for 30–60 minutes, until firm but not brittle. Push a lollipop stick
into each cake pop, then chill for an additional 10 minutes.

4. Coarsely chop the remaining milk chocolate and melt as above, then
remove from the heat. Dip a cake pop into the chocolate, turning it until
coated. Lift it from the bowl, letting the excess drip back into the bowl,
and place it in a cup or glass. Sprinkle with the chocolate sprinkles.
Repeat with the remaining cake pops. Chill or let stand in a cool place
until the chocolate has set.

Chocolate "ice-cream" cones

Makes: 16
Prep: 40 minutes, plus setting
Cook: 2–3 minutes

4½ oz/125 g milk chocolate, coarsely chopped

scant 1 cup heavy cream

2 tbsp vanilla sugar

chocolate and rainbow sugar sprinkles, to decorate

MOUSSE

7 oz/200 g semisweet chocolate, coarsely chopped

4 tbsp water

2 egg whites

2 tbsp superfine sugar

These mini chocolate cones are filled with a delicious chocolate mousse and topped with swirls of whipped cream. Unlike regular ice creams, they won't melt if left out of the freezer!

1. Line a baking sheet with parchment paper. To shape the cones, cut 8 circles of parchment paper using a 7-inch/18-cm plate or cake pan as a guide. Fold the circles in half, then cut them in half just to one side of the fold. Shape each semicircle into a cone so the straight edges meet to create a cone of double thickness paper, then secure in place with adhesive tape.

2. Put the milk chocolate in a heatproof bowl, set the bowl over a pan of gently simmering water, and heat until melted. Place a teaspoon of melted chocolate into a cone so that it's about one-third full, and spread the chocolate up the sides using a pastry brush. Invert it onto the baking sheet and chill for at least 30 minutes, until set.

3. To make the mousse, put the semisweet chocolate and water in a heatproof bowl, set the bowl over a pan of gently simmering water, and heat until melted. Whisk the egg whites in a clean mixing bowl until forming peaks. Whisk in the superfine sugar, a little at a time. Tip the melted chocolate onto the whites and fold together with a spatula. Spoon the mousse into the cones and chill for 1 hour.

4. Whip the cream with the vanilla sugar until just forming peaks. Put it into a small pastry bag fitted with a ½-inch/1-cm star tip. Peel the paper from the cones and pipe swirls of cream on top. Scatter with sprinkles.

Double chocolate whoopie pies

Makes: 12–14
Prep: 25 minutes, plus cooling
Cook: 10 minutes

5 tbsp lightly salted butter, softened

⅔ cup light brown sugar

1 egg

1 tsp vanilla extract

1 cup all-purpose flour

½ tsp baking soda

heaping ⅓ cup unsweetened cocoa

⅓ cup buttermilk

FILLING

7 oz/200 g milk chocolate, coarsely chopped

heaping ½ cup unsalted butter, softened

⅔ cup confectioners' sugar

2½ oz/70 g semisweet chocolate, coarsely chopped

chocolate sprinkles, optional

Quench your chocolate craving with these moist, homemade whoopies; they're so good they'll be gone before you know it!

1. Preheat the oven to 400°F/200°C. Line 2 baking sheets with parchment paper. Put the lightly salted butter, light brown sugar, egg, and vanilla in a mixing bowl and beat together with an electric handheld whisk until the mixture is thickened and pale.

2. Sift the flour, baking soda, and cocoa into a separate mixing bowl. Add half of this mixture and half of the buttermilk to the butter mixture. Stir with a spatula or large metal spoon. Once combined, add the remaining flour mixture and buttermilk and carefully stir again.

3. Put the batter into a large pastry bag fitted with a ½-inch/1-cm plain tip (see page 8). Pipe small mounds onto the baking sheets, slicing off the peaks with a small knife and spacing the mounds about 2 inches/5 cm apart to allow for expansion.

4. Bake in the preheated oven for 10 minutes, or until risen and just firm to the touch, switching over the baking sheets halfway through baking. Let stand on the sheets for 5 minutes, then transfer to a wire rack to cool.

5. For the filling, put the milk chocolate in a heatproof bowl, set the bowl over a saucepan of gently simmering water, and heat until melted. Let stand to cool slightly. Put the unsalted butter and confectioners' sugar in a mixing bowl and beat with an electric handheld whisk until light and fluffy. Stir the melted chocolate into the butter mixture until evenly combined.

6. Sandwich the whoopie pies together in pairs with the filling. Melt the semisweet chocolate as above, then drizzle a little of it over each whoopie pie. Scatter with the sprinkles, if using. Let stand in a cool place to firm up for a couple of hours.

Gingerbread and vanilla whoopie pies

Makes: 14
Prep: 25 minutes, plus cooling
Cook: 10 minutes

1 egg

⅓ cup light brown sugar

1 tbsp molasses

3 tbsp lightly salted butter, melted

5 tbsp milk

scant 1¼ cups all-purpose flour

½ tsp baking soda

1½ tsp ground ginger

½ tsp ground allspice

FILLING

scant ½ cup cream cheese

1 tbsp unsalted butter, softened

1 tsp vanilla extract

scant ½ cup confectioners' sugar, plus extra for dusting

1 tsp boiling water

These whoopies have a distinctive gingerbread flavor, perfect for wintertime comfort eating!

1. Preheat the oven to 350°F/180°C. Line 2 baking sheets with parchment paper. Put the egg, light brown sugar, and molasses in a mixing bowl and beat together with an electric handheld whisk until thickened and foamy. Beat in the lightly salted butter and milk.

2. Sift the flour, baking soda, ginger, and allspice into the bowl and stir with a wooden spoon to make a soft paste.

3. Spoon teaspoons of the mixture onto the baking sheets, flattening them slightly so each spoonful is about 1¼ inches/3 cm in diameter. Space the spoonfuls about 2 inches/5 cm apart to allow for expansion.

4. Bake in the preheated oven for 10 minutes, or until risen and firm to the touch, switching over the baking sheets halfway through baking. Let stand on the sheets for 5 minutes, then transfer to a wire rack to cool.

5. For the filling, put the cream cheese, unsalted butter, vanilla, and confectioners' sugar in a mixing bowl and beat together with an electric handheld whisk until smooth and creamy. Beat in the boiling water to soften. Sandwich the whoopie pies together in pairs with the filling. Let stand in a cool place to firm up for a couple of hours, then dust with confectioners' sugar.

Index